GET to the TOP

GET to the TOP

The ten rules for social success

SUHEL SETH

EBURY PRESS

An imprint of Penguin Random House

EBURY PRESS

USA | Canada | UK | Ireland | Australia
New Zealand | India | South Africa | China | Singapore

Ebury Press is part of the Penguin Random House group of companies whose addresses can be found at global.penguinrandomhouse.com

Published by Penguin Random House India Pvt. Ltd
4th Floor, Capital Tower 1, MG Road,
Gurugram 122 002, Haryana, India

Penguin Random House India

First published in Ebury Press by Random House India 2011
This paperback edition published 2014

10 9 8 7 6 5 4 3 2

ISBN 9788184006407

Typeset by Le Studio Graphique

Printed at Repro India Limited

www.penguin.co.in

FSC www.fsc.org MIX Paper from responsible sources FSC® C047271

This is a legitimate digitally printed version of the book and therefore might not have certain extra finishing on the cover.

Dedicated to

Shub and Jogendra Seth, my wonderful parents...
For bringing me into this world and then tolerating me

CONTENTS

PART ONE

HOW TO DRAW PEOPLE TO YOU

Friendships happen when people are drawn to each other. How do you make yourself a more attractive person to others? You have got to have the ability to make people laugh, make them remember you, and yes, you must entertain them. And you can only do so with a blend of knowledge and humour.

I have two simple rules about this.

RULE 1

The self-development rule

(be interested and interesting)

WHAT THIS RULE WILL TEACH YOU

- Enrich your mind

- Understand the difference between being intelligent and being interesting—and why the latter will ultimately get you further

- Appreciate the importance of being multidimensional

Okay, here's the deal. You can't be socially successful if you're not interested in things—not unless you're as gorgeous as Bollywood beauty Aishwarya Rai or as wealthy as entrepreneur Analjit Singh, in which case your money and good looks can do an 'Open sesame!' into the world of social success for you. For the rest of us ordinary mortals, being unidimensional is an issue. Frankly, it can often be an issue even if you are beautiful and rich.

The self-development rule is number one because it is the most important. *Be interested in everything*, or in as many things as you can manage. And the easiest way to learn interesting things is by reading as widely as you can. In the last six months, I have read everything I could get my hands on, from *Marie Claire's* cover story on Deepika Padukone to whether the Middle East can build stable democracies in the *Economist*. In my library at home, you'll find F. Scott Fitzgerald's great classic, *The Great Gatsby*, Tina Brown's gossipy account of Princess Diana, *The Diana Chronicles*, and Ramachandra Guha's masterly history of modern India, *India After Gandhi*. As a result, I can banter about Deepika's new hairstyle with my client's daughters and argue about world politics at a think tank dinner. Trust me when I say both hold me in good stead.

The reason I read is because it helps me talk. Simple. The more I know, the more I can engage people in conversation. In fact, a lot of what I do involves talking. I speak at conferences, I talk to CEOs, make presentations, and address management teams and students alike. For most of you too, talking is likely to be a key part of your work and play. You may not do much public speaking but you'll find that the more widely you read, the easier it is to hold conversations, even at a casual, intimate level. Talking helps create a brand value for oneself. I am able to articulate things that would otherwise escape others. I am also able to deliver one-liners in a manner that they will be remembered. My involvement with college theatre and debating as a young man has helped me a great deal in being able to express my thoughts and opinions but it's reading that has given me the substance.

I have always said that public speaking as an art form can take you places, and it almost always does. President Barack Obama is not as famous today for his health care reforms, as he is for his speeches.

To this day, the bestselling book at the venerable bookstore Hatchards, in London, is a collection of the speeches of Britain's former Prime Minister, Winston Churchill. Here at home, Pandit Jawaharlal Nehru's 'tryst with destiny' speech still brings tears to people's eyes. These men used speaking to connect emotionally and intellectually with people and communicate something of themselves.

Remember, whether it's you, me, Gandhi or Obama, ultimately, we are all brands. Human brands perhaps, but brands nonetheless. This means that each of us has qualities (and disadvantages) that are uniquely ours. That's what people buy into most of the time. You don't get invited out because the person extending the invitation liked your clothes. They may have eyes for your money but that appeal wears off after a time. After all, when was the last time you wanted to sit down for dinner with the freshly minted paan masala owner? Or for that matter the shady electronics trader or your local bootlegger? It's not the absence of wealth that makes them unappealing but the fact that they don't make much of an impression in most circles. You make an impression when you've created a brand for yourself and the best way to create this brand is with words.

Knowledge is the social fodder that feeds today's information-driven world. You have to read and you have to be able to talk. That's why you need to make books your best friends. They will help you get very far and they're the only friends that will last both social and economic downturns. You may decide to drop an industrialist from your friends' circle or simply forget him because he's suddenly become poor or irrelevant but authors and poets will always be welcome. Knowledge is recession-proof and has universal appeal. Women are as impressed by a well-read individual as men are. A little-acknowledged fact is that ultimately, women love men with brains. This is why Marilyn Monroe married Arthur Miller, the playwright and not some *Sports Illustrated* model with ugly biceps or some millionaire.

The man who taught me this simple (yet profound) truth was my first boss Ram Ray.

Ram, for those of you who don't know, is a legend in Indian advertising. He is the founder and CEO of the ad agency Response, and before that, he had an illustrious career with J. Walter Thompson, one of the biggest advertising agencies in the world. When I joined Response in 1986, it was known for its seminal campaigns for brands like Jenson and Nicholson (although it wasn't responsible for creating that great tagline, 'Whenever you think of colour, think of us'. That was by Arun Nehru, the paint company's former CEO) and Boroline. Boroline became the quintessential Bengali ad. It essentially said that in every Bengali's life, there had to be a chakar (servant), kukur (pet), pukur (pond), and Boroline. Response was also the agency that launched the soap Aramusk. We were the first agency to brand a soap not on cleanliness, but on sex appeal. Lust versus lather.

As for Ram, well, he seemed to us to be more like a rotund professor at a suburban college in midwest America than an advertising agency boss in central Kolkata. He is a portly, bespectacled man with a bearing that may remind you of waddling ducks. He is also a man with many passions. He loves Kolkata, literature, cinema, photography, typography, art, crafts, food and the Internet. He was probably the second person to get himself an Apple computer after Steve Jobs. He's also someone who won't have his Bloody Mary without a celery stick in it and will make sure the glass is properly rimmed with salt. Now of course in Delhi, they use Swarovski sticks.

Ram was both generous and patient with his employees. He had a library that he was proud of and was equally happy to let all of us who worked for him dip into it. I was a mere management trainee and Ram needn't have been that indulgent. But then, Ram knew we were the soldiers who were facing client ranks. If we looked smart, so did Response. I remember many a time I would pick up a book that had nothing to do with marketing but would instead be about the history of fonts. Yes, fonts that you use for writing. I could then have a conversation with my art director on his subject rather than mine. In the process, my work would get done before anyone else's, in addition to me having gained some unexpected knowledge, which, again, never kills you!

Ram didn't just encourage us to read widely, but also, like him, to have as many interests as possible. Response sponsored my play *Bhutto* and designed its brochure because he approved of my being passionate about theatre, for example. As a result, the greatest lessons Ram taught me were all outside of work. During the day, we worked as advertising executives, slogging over briefs and taglines, but post-sunset, Ram would conjure a different world for all of us. From discussing typography to waxing forth on Ayn Rand, he would create an adda like I had never seen before. We were dazzled. This is what my colleagues and I looked forward to. There was nothing more stimulating than ending a day with the guarantee that you'd learn even more tomorrow. This has always been my mantra since. *You will never know enough. Don't be insecure about this. Rather, be secure in the belief that you will learn more and be prepared to learn all the time. The mind must be an ever-absorbing sponge.*

I remember having French onion soup with Ram at the newly opened Conclave, Kolkata's first upscale restaurant, where we spent hours discussing the manner in which the onion had to be peeled. Our conversations weren't just about gourmet food. I have fond memories of arguing with him about where to get the best jhaal muri in town, while discussing the launch of Frooti. (This goes back to my earlier point: be interested in everything).

Ram also taught me the need to think tangentially. Tangential thinking was made famous by Edward De Bono in his book, *Six Thinking Hats*, and it is jargon for thinking out of the box. Ram encouraged this to a fault. The only way you can think tangentially is if you have an open mind and enough knowledge to back your ideas up. The latter will come from reading and, more critically, from listening and absorbing. We would use it to find ways out of Kolkata's famed traffic snarls and also for client solutions. This is what gave me unbridled joy: to work with a man who cared for no conventions, no borders. All he wanted was young, unfettered minds, anchored in integrity and logic.

The reason why I am labouring over the point about Ram is because he shaped me into the man I am today and many of my interests arise in part because of his passions. There are two sub-rules to this.

.... SUB-RULE 1 ....

Get a mentor

Apart from reading, another way to cultivate interests is to get yourself a mentor or to surround yourself with people who have lots of interests. Mentors are different from people you would ordinarily think of as benefactors. You don't have to announce someone as your mentor but it is important, even silently, to accept someone as the same. Mentors help you stay the course. They also help you recognize the pitfalls from moments of triumph. They help you learn new things and thanks to all this, they are the ultimate accessory. Very few of us are lucky enough to find mentors like Ram was to me but there will always be someone around you who will have experience beyond yours and know about things that you don't. Celebrate that, and be prepared to sit at your mentor's feet and learn, rather than be obnoxious and believe you know it all.

Remember, mentoring is not a twenty-first century concept. Krishna was not Arjuna's god; he was his mentor. In that famous conversation, held on a chariot, there were many life lessons that Arjuna received from Krishna, but not once did Krishna force Arjuna to adopt them. That is the hallmark of a true mentor. He shows you many paths but ultimately, it is your journey and the destination is one that you set for yourself. This is how mentors are different from benefactors. Mentors show you the way. Unlike benefactors, they don't hold your hand or carry you all the way to your goals.

SUB SUB-RULE

Say thank you

Many years ago, I was invited to speak on the occasion of the sixtieth anniversary of the Advertising Club of Kolkata. I began my speech by saying that I was where I was in life, thanks to Ram Ray. I could see Ram was moved. But more than him, the many advertising folks, who would normally pretend they did everything on their own and were individual icons, were affected by my declaration. My dear friend Piyush Pandey, now a creative legend in the advertising business, will always credit the genius of O&M's creative bigwig, Suresh Mullick. It does not make you smaller or any less important if you have the courage to salute the people who have helped you become what you are. *Gratitude is an important ingredient of strong character. The more you express it, the better off you will be*. I also publicly acknowledge Uma Gajapati Raju and Ramesh Sharma, the film and TV producers, for introducing me to Delhi. I always thank God for how Delhi's über hostess Mala Singh and her husband Jugnu, as well as journalist Shekhar Gupta and his wife Neelam embraced me as family when I first moved to the city. It was

Shekhar first and then M.J. Akbar who encouraged me to write. For those opportunities I have always been grateful, as I have been to Rajdeep Sardesai for being the first to invite me to a public debate on television when he was still with NDTV. The same goes for Aveek Sarkar who has continued to publish my weekly agony uncle column, titled 'Survival Strategies', in *The Telegraph* for the last fifteen years.

....

But to return to the point—don't be a bloody bore. It really is the greatest social crime you can commit (for a longer list go to the Appendix). What made Ram inspiring wasn't only that he was good at his job, but that he was interested in so many other things. He wanted to surround himself with interesting people, not just bright people. And there is a difference between the two. *You are not successful if you are bright. You are successful if you are interesting. Usually, your interests make you interesting.*

That's the great thing about this rule. You can develop yourself even if you aren't the funniest or the liveliest person in the room. Wouldn't you rather spend the cocktail talking to someone who is a marathon runner or who goes on Himalayan expeditions each year, than to a banker who is obsessed only by the stock market? I know I would. After all, the first secret to social success is to stand out. I am not suggesting that you suddenly audition for the next play or force a debate in your colony. All I'm saying is that it pays to be multidimensional and well read. Find things outside of work about which you feel passionately. There's so much happening out there, so you have no excuses. You don't need to be interested in just worthy causes. I love cars, books, travelling, food, theatre, pretty women, politics, business, marketing, gossip; and I indulge my passions as much as possible.

Each year I take three months off. It is absolutely non-negotiable and my clients never complain. Those three months allow me to indulge in all my pleasures, from wine to William Shakespeare. I alternate between travelling to places as different as Spit in Croatia to Venice in Italy. I meet old friends and make new ones. I do silly things that don't generally make it to anyone's 'must do' list and above all, one of those three months is spent with my parents. These things are important in life. They help you see a world beyond the one at your desk. Walk around the churches in Prague and listen to their music. It will open your eyes to unknown pleasures. Take a trip to Dharamshala and you will see beauty that is unimaginable. Go to Munnar and see the amazing work that the Tatas are doing in the social sector and you will begin to have hope in India. The key is that your involvement cannot be cursory. It must be complete and utterly passionate. Find things to love. *Life is not about being simply interested in things. It is about being involved with them.*

I have always told colleagues and friends that their place on this planet is as human beings and not plodders. Bulls work, so do oxen. But men and women are destined for more than just a routine job. The more you do your job to the exclusion of everything else, the more stifled and less attractive you will be. Such is life. Develop interests that are as tangential as possible. Go see plays; watch as many movies as you can, even Bollywood will do. Go to the opera and if you don't want to do this esoteric stuff, then go travel and observe human behaviour. Read as much as you can; develop an interest in music. Move beyond that office and that wretched job. You will become saner, and a better and more valued professional. One day you will all finish doing your jobs. What will seize you then? How will you spend your days and evenings? For self-preservation alone, if for nothing else, develop a bunch of interests. This is what will last.

MY MANTRAS

•

Read as if there is no tomorrow and read everything from the banal to the sublime. There are gems in both.

•

Thank the lord if you get a mentor and remember to thank the mentor as well.

•

Create for yourself an interest prism and look at life through your interests and not just in the unidimensional way you may be doing presently.

•

Learning to be interesting is as important as being hardworking and bright.

•

And remember, it's not even about external success in the ultimate analysis, it is about enriching yourself.

RULE 2

The impact rule

(have an opinion)

WHAT THIS RULE WILL TEACH YOU

- How to impress important people
- What to have an opinion on—and what not to
- How to ensure that your opinions don't make you enemies

Rule 2 follows on from Rule 1. You read widely, you have varied interests but do you have an opinion? Are you brave (or perhaps foolish) enough to voice it? It's not about being right or wrong. It's about taking a stand. You need to have an opinion on certain matters even if it means ruffling a few feathers, and they need to go beyond your professional domain. *The key to social success is to have an opinion.*

I don't get invited to parties because of my looks or my wealth. I get invited (or so I believe) because people want to hear what I have to say or at least because they know I will not shy away from speaking my mind. Will the next-gen Indian prefer football to cricket? Is Shah Rukh Khan going to beat Aamir Khan at the box office this year? Should the Indian media go online? Ought Nitish Kumar project himself as prime minister in the next general elections?

It is not important what your opinion is. What is important is that you do not come across as someone who has nothing to say and is happy either being silent or a fence sitter. Many a time when I am speaking abroad, I am tempted to deflect the attention from unpleasant issues. For instance, the last time I was addressing the Harvard Club in New York, someone from the audience asked me about corruption in India. I could have easily deflected or dodged that question. But then I took it head-on and said there is as much corruption in India as there is in the United States and historically, corruption emerges from unbridled capitalism. There was much applause and I felt I had done the right thing by being honest and upfront.

On my part, I love going to homes and places where I know there will be intelligent discussion and opinions will be laid bare. I may not agree with them but I know it will not be a room of airheads with the only noise coming from clinking wineglasses. Nor would I notice someone unless they have something interesting to say. In times such as the ones we live in, hurried as they are, people expect to meet to either learn something or be entertained intellectually. This is why it is critical to blend knowledge with articulation. No one cares how bright you are unless you make an impression with your intelligence.

If you're a smart, ambitious young man or woman reading this book in the hope of getting some tips to get to the top, then keep this in mind: *the one sure way to get someone's attention is to have a strong stand on issues*. As a young man in Kolkata, I made many friends amongst people who were at least thrice (if not four times) my age, only because I could strike up a conversation and keep them entertained. One of these was the great Russi Mody, then the chairman of Tata Steel. I was a mere accounts executive with Ogilvy & Mather and he was known as the 'Emperor of Tata Steel'.

They don't make them like Russi Mody any more. The man was a bon vivant. He would fly to Mumbai just to have dinner, at the drop of a hat; always spent summers in the south of France; loved his champagnes and cigars, and was a regular at the Ascot races in England. I adored the man and he liked my outspokenness. And so, despite our differences in age and status, I was lucky enough to spend a great deal of time with him when I was a young man. I am proud to say that our friendship today is over twenty years long.

I remember one evening in particular. It was a Sunday, the evenings I normally spent with my parents. I was home when I got a call from Russi saying he wanted me to come over and had prepared my favourite egg sandwiches. So I got into the car and reached the Tata Centre. Barely had I arrived when his majordomo, Roy, told me we were all going to the airport. I was aghast. I hadn't told my mother I would not be dining with them nor was I wearing particularly decent clothes, but off we went to Mumbai where Russi had invited the head honchos from the Tata Group, such as the well-known lawyer, Nani Palkhivala and Darbari Seth, a key JRD aide, at his Altamount Road home. We had dinner and then flew back to Kolkata at 3.30 am.

The next morning I arrived at the Tata Centre where, as luck would have it, I was making a presentation to Russi, my companion from the previous evening. During my presentation, I happened to yawn. Russi looked me in the eye and asked if I'd had a late night. He was no longer my friend in the room. He was my client. I simply apologized and continued. Later that day, my MD, Mani Ayer of Ogilvy, caught me yawning too. I could have told him that I had gone out with Russi the night before and my MD would have been only too happy. But I did not. Russi respected the fact that I was not taking advantage of our friendship and had maintained a professional distance, as I should, which helped our relationship even more.

Now there are some sub-rules to this and I'll get to them in a bit. But let's stay here for the moment. You might think from what I have said that the more outlandish your views, the more attention they will attract. Wrong. An opinion is not provocation. They sometimes seem alike but they couldn't be more different. Take for instance my well-known views about Narendra Modi. I have often written against him for the atrocities that happened in Godhra but I was also the first so-called liberal to praise the enormous good he's done to Gujarat as an administrator. I have been pilloried for both but I have never changed my stance. Nor am I about to in the future, unless Modi does an about-turn. Your opinions about things should be deep rooted; they should be things that have arisen out of your convictions. And you must not simply see them as a useful tool for social advancement. *Everyone ought to know where they stand.* Life is not a train timetable, to be hurriedly glanced at, then abandoned as you rush to catch the train. You should know what you believe in and for which train you have a ticket.

Having an opinion shows intellectual honesty. I think, for example, that people have judged George W. Bush, Jr harshly and that history will see him with kinder eyes. He genuinely believed that the war on Iraq was necessary and so he did what he had to do. The world may not agree with him. The liberals in the New Yorks of the world see him as a pariah but then you have to go deeper into things than what's made out in the media. Your opinions have to be yours ultimately. They cannot be those of some editor.

Today, most people don't want to risk an opinion. We all wish to be popular and non-confrontational but you never can be everyone's favourite and it's not worth it to even try. There are no risks in having a contrarian view, provided you can back it up with logic and conviction, and stay the course. Many a time, people offer an opinion and change it the next instant just because it is not fashionable but you should take your stand more seriously. One opinion can stop a mining contract. It can make you worthy of treason and famous. Look at author and activist Arundhati Roy or Shabir Shah who has been campaigning for Kashmir's independence so vociferously. Even though I am not an ardent fan of Arundhati Roy, I strongly believe she has every right to her opinion, no matter how contrarian it is. *Here's a counter-mantra: you have to be sharp enough to have an opinion of your own and magnanimous to accept a completely different one from someone else.*

I must admit that I am guilty of often having too many opinions. GQ called me 'TV's bad boy' in a recent article and I suppose they are right. But let me assure you that I always play it straight and I say what I mean. This has cost me a few friendships. Some years ago, for example, I wrote an article in which I argued that the state should target rich cocaine users and not the poor drug dealers if they really wanted to curb the drug problem. I got a call from Priya Paul of the Apeejay Group, one of my oldest friends from Kolkata, protesting about what I had written. But for me it was not about any individual. It was about the issue itself, which is the double standards in the state's attitude towards law enforcement with regard to drugs. I don't have regrets over principled stands but I know that these will jeopardize some of my relationships. You should be aware of this too.

Yet what's more surprising is to see how many friendships *have not* been damaged (at least not irreparably) by my opinions. In a *Brunch* cover story, I criticized the Bachchans on the break-up between Abhishek Bachchan and Karisma Kapoor and then on Jaya Bachchan's entry into the Rajya Sabha. I admit I was naïve and stupid and had got carried away. It upset them a great deal as you can imagine; even Amar Singh wrote a huge article in response. After 26/11, Amitabh Bachchan sent me a lovely SMS just after I had finished speaking on Times Now. I was very touched. It showed a lot of grace on his part. Today, I am deeply fond of the family and have spent many special moments with them. Mr L.K. Advani was similarly upset at an article I wrote criticizing him but later asked me to review his memoirs. And I did. In fact, although I liked his book, it did not prevent me from asking him uncomfortable questions at the *Hindustan Times* Summit some months later!

The reason why the Bachchans and Mr Advani forgave me is that they know I had no motivation for my critiques. My opinions aren't based on any personal or politicking agenda and, while they can sometimes hurt, they are not malicious. So even though many people feel my sting, most eventually either forget the barb or excuse me. And this brings me to the all-important sub-rules.

SUB-RULE 1

No agenda

This is an extension of the last point and it is as important as the rule itself. The one thing you need to be careful of is that your opinions don't arise from any hidden motivation. You don't slam your director's business strategy at the post-work hangout because the two of you have had a quarrel but because you genuinely believe that he's making the wrong move. For example, when I speak about Coca-Cola on television, I always declare that I am their consultant. As I've said before, opinions aren't provocations and they need to be deeply rooted in what you believe. The day your opinions begin to look like judgements or planted statements, you're dead.

SUB-RULE 2

Curb your opinion

There are some areas where you shouldn't have too many opinions. Other people's sex lives, especially their sexuality, is one such example. Religion too is a sensitive and deeply personal area. You may not think much of the godman an acquaintance is obsessed with, but you don't need to make it an issue. Politics is also a touchy area. Have an opinion on the impact their politics have, but not on the person (more on this in the next rule).

SUB-RULE 3

After hours only

Opinions are for after hours. Having strong opinions may or may not get you ahead at work. I would suggest you don't have opinions from 9 am to 6 pm because during that time, people are looking towards getting work done or hearing a professional opinion, and not being regaled by your beliefs. Recognize and respect that. There may be many instances when you don't agree with your client's views or his business strategy and to give a professional opinion is fine. To give a moral one, however, is silly. I, for instance, have always attacked Unilever for promoting fair skin as something that gives you an advantage in the workplace through the advertisements for their product Fair & Lovely. But that is a moral stand and not a professional one.

SUB-RULE 4

Change is okay

The art of expressing an opinion also entails the ability to change it. There is no better phrase than 'I was wrong', when you have an opinion that may either be completely wrong or inappropriate. But you can't sound wishy-washy. Even your altered opinion should have limbs on which it can stand. Many years ago, I had written about Ratan Tata in *The Indian Express* for summarily ensuring the departure of Russi Modi from Tata Steel and argued that he would be the Tata Group's downfall. The years have proven my words very, very wrong. Ratan Tata has taken the Group from strength to strength and many Tata companies are my clients today. I freely admit that I was wrong in my opinion of Ratan Tata. Today, I know how blessed the Tata Group is to have someone like Ratan at the helm: he blends a strong value system with very sharp intellect and every decision of his, in hindsight, has been one which has not only made the Tatas very profitable but the nation equally proud: be it the Nano, the acquisition of Corus and JLR or for that matter his continued support to (and the establishment of) the Tata Medical Center, the first ever cancer hospital in eastern India despite the famous stand-off with Mamata Banerjee in Singur.

....

Ultimately, *the secret to expressing an opinion intelligently is to ensure that it doesn't cause irreparable offence*. You want to make friends, not enemies. This is a fine art. There are a number of things to keep in mind here. First, delivery is key. Second, don't become what I call an 'opinion terrorist', which means—don't foist your opinions on others; just have them and own them without disrespecting anyone. It is, as I have said earlier, also important to respect others' opinions as well.

I learnt this from my debating days in Kolkata. As I have already told you, I had two great passions while growing up—theatre and debating. Let me tell you, I didn't just love debating, I was also bloody good at it. I won every possible debate! I even won the Ashutosh Mukherjee Memorial debate (the city's best known college debate) three times in a row and the award they gave me in recognition of that achievement still sits proudly in my study. It may seem like an inconsequential student award but it's my most treasured prize. The secret to my success was learning to be flexible. Often, to test your debating skills, you would be given the side of the motion you had to speak on, just ten minutes before the debate began. This taught me an invaluable lesson. You don't just need to know both sides of an argument but also respect each side equally. Debating teaches you to respect dissent and everyone needs to cultivate that quality. There have been many instances when during a debate I have changed my stance and audaciously enough, offered a reason for doing so and won the debate.

I have never agreed with my friend Arun Jaitley on Narendra Modi; nor do I see eye to eye with my friend Romi Chopra, a close friend of the Gandhi family, on Indira and Rajiv Gandhi. I genuinely believe that Modi made a colossal blunder in the manner in which he handled the situation after the terrible incidents of violence in Godhra. I am no investigating agency and will not rush to conclusions as to who did it but Modi, for all his other skills, has let the perception stick of him being a mass murderer. As for Rajiv Gandhi, I feel he let an entire nation down. All the remarkable good that he did with liberalization was dwarfed by the shadow of Bofors. Yes, taking a political stand is tricky but not if you are supporting an ideology rather than a belief. Let me illustrate: the Emergency was one of India's darkest hours. It did not matter which side of the spectrum you were on: you just had to oppose this attack on our freedom. Similarly, with any brand of communalism. Be it Hindu or Muslim or Sikh.

Both Arun and Romi have often fiercely opposed me—yet we all know that my opinions about their friends doesn't affect our relationship. Here's another example: take my ties with the Confederation of Indian Industry (CII). CII apologized to Narendra Modi when two of its members, Deepak Parekh and Anu Aga, criticized his actions in Godhra. I wrote against CII for making such an apology but the institution didn't ask me to leave their national council on which I used to serve at the time. This is why I prefer Delhi to Mumbai. Delhi, for all its Punjabi bling, can have salon conversations and at the heart of a salon conversation is the idea that people voice opinions while allowing others to have their own.

The bottom line is that it is essential to cultivate the art of the apolitical opinion. You may take an ideological stand but it must be issue based. For instance, I have always said in my speeches and articles that India cannot afford to be divided on religion and that hatred can pull a country down economically. It is not a political advantage, as many see it to be. Today no one can accuse me of being pro-Congress or pro-BJP. I attack both their policies. At my parties, you will see Jyotiraditya Scindia or Kamal Nath and Praful Patel or for that matter, editors with completely contrarian views—be it Rajdeep Sardesai or Arnab Goswami.

Before we move to the next rule, let's look at the things about which you should have opinions. Given how gripped Indians are by politics and culture, it would be wise to have an opinion on both. We should have an opinion on electoral reforms since it gives us a chance to decide whether thugs will participate in our democracy. We must take a stand against the use and abuse of religion in this country. Similarly, it is always prudent to have an opinion about your professional domain but not in isolation. Link it to nation building if you can. I have always spoken about brands and marketing in the context of India and the Indian. For me 'Brand India' can only exist if I understand the hues and colours of my country from both a social and commercial perspective. Not in isolation, ever.

I also see the advantage of new online vehicles for expressing opinions such as Twitter. But then, like with every medium, you should use it strategically. Use it to say something substantive but be prepared to face criticism and occasionally an onslaught of intellectual abuse. *Remember, these media tools are relevant and rewarding if they are used as a means of dialogue and not just dissemination.* I believe, for all that has happened, Shashi Tharoor uses Twitter very well, as does Vijay Mallya and even Anand Mahindra. A bit of self promotion and company promotion on Twitter is only expected and they have interesting tweets.

MY MANTRAS

•

Having opinions is the key to getting noticed.

•

People need to be like sanitary napkins: absorb all opinions but not colour the issues.

•

Think like a debater: respect the other side of your argument.

•

Delivery is key: opinions should make you friends not enemies.

PART TWO

HOW TO MAKE FRIENDS

The first two rules will help you develop your personality. Once you've started living and thinking according to them, it's time to use your skills in the real battle—making interesting, new friends. In the second part, I'll reveal all my trade secrets. So pay attention. I'll tell you what qualities you need to make friends and how to manage your relationships with powerful people. Remember, you are not the only one who is befriending powerful people. The whole world and their mother is doing the same. The act of befriending is not the issue, it's what you do with the friendship that counts.

RULE 3

The popularity rule
(don't judge people)

WHAT THIS RULE WILL TEACH YOU

- The secret to throwing a good party
- To look for the right things when making new friends
- The necessity of older and younger friends

I often get asked why my parties are so much fun. The answer is simple (and more on parties in the Appendix)—I have the most eclectic group of people at my home at any event. I very consciously mix up politicians, industrialists, journalists, pretty girls (an indispensable ingredient), actors, models, old friends, socialites, thirty-somethings and eighty-somethings.

What's the secret? I like them all. And because I like them, they like me. This, my friends, is the real secret of popularity. I like them, not for who they are but for what they are like. My guest lists don't change with political or economic winds. I have had almost the same set of people at my parties since I can remember.[1] Over the years I have simply added to that guest list but I have rarely subtracted. The trick is to not judge people and accept them on their own terms. Judge their opinions, but not them as people (there are, of course, exceptions; see sub-rule 1).

[1] Nor do I succumb to, what I call, social terrorism. Often I get calls from people on the day of my dinner, asking if I am throwing a party. The caller hopes to get invited but if they are not a fit with my guest list for the evening, I don't invite them and tell them clearly why I can't.

This is why the former lawyer and now BJP leader, Arun Jaitley, is a dear friend of mine even though we are on opposite sides of the political spectrum. I don't like BJP's right-wing politics but I like Arun for his human values. He's an intelligent, straightforward, witty man and a loyal friend. I enjoy his company, we often holiday together and I trust him implicitly. That is the basis of our friendship. I have many friends like Arun, men and women who are utterly different from me.

If I like a person, I accept their opinions and actions even if I disagree with them (see Rule 2). When Vinod Mehta carried a recording of my (inconsequential) conversation with Niira Radia in *Outlook*, everyone thought I would be upset. Not at all. He remains a dear and valued friend. He was doing his job and I will keep my friendship intact. What I respect about Vinod is that he did not call me to warn me in advance nor did I raise a ruckus with him once the magazine was out. Why should I?

I have an eclectic friends' circle because of this attitude and all sorts of people have come together in my house for parties. In Kolkata, I would bring together people as disparate as industrialist Russi

Mody and musician Ananda Shankar. In Mumbai, the cartoonist R.K. Laxman would rub shoulders with filmmaker Subhash Ghai. In Delhi, I don't favour one political party over the other. In fact, someone once joked that my parties were like being in parliament when it was not in session.

One part of the Popularity Rule is about accepting people on their own terms. The other aspect is regarding everyone as equal. Unlike other homes, whoever enters my house does so on the same footing as the next person. I couldn't be bothered if he is a minister or a shy, young lawyer, a socialite, or a Nobel Prize winner. They leave their ego, power, and riches at the door. As a result, my parties are an unthreatening environment to people, particularly important ones, because I let people be and I never invite any form of press to my home for coverage. Plus, people also know that there will be good food (always served on time. See Appendix), excellent alcohol, and general bonhomie. No one is watching anyone or hanging on to every word uttered, unless they're star struck by the gathering, which is unlikely if they're anyone of importance themselves.

So when you go out to a social event or have people over, leave your judgement at the door. And if you can't do that, make sure you don't show it.

SUB-RULE 1

What to judge

Do judge people on their values. I would never have an arms dealer or a person who has been to jail at my house. There are many powerful and important people whom I would never invite to my home as I think they completely lack values. Nor would I go to their homes.

The advantage of being non-judgemental is that it opens you up to engaging with all kinds of people and experiences. I like hanging out with businessmen as much as I like hanging out with ravishing bimbos. I often finish a gruelling debate on television and rush off to a page 3 party directly after. A study in contrasts? No, just a great way to unwind. Sometimes it's fun to merge with the furniture, not engage in conversation and admire the curvaceous forms of beautiful women. I love moving from the sublime to the inane. And as a marketing man, I know it's vital not to cocoon myself with one type of person.

Besides, dishonesty is likely to get to you even if nothing else does. I have often been taunted about being a fixture on page 3. Well, what's the harm? I love the good things in life and I have earned it the hard way. The trick is to live life on your terms and never to do what society tells you to or expects of you. People, many a time, are plain envious. At least I am not like some fancy industrialist who is cheating on his dove-like wife and going around strutting the global stage as a corporate messiah.

I was born non-judgemental and have always loved meeting people. So this rule came easily to me. Later as I entered the world of marketing, my natural inclination merged with my profession. I was good at my job because I put myself in the shoes of the customer. Meeting people was the only way I could get an insight into the ever-evolving human behaviour and stay relevant and on my toes. This is why I spend hours with my nephews. I love them but also find their company completely energizing. I love hearing about the latest video game they are into, what the cool music is, what everyone is wearing.

As a young man, I was the opposite. I hated hanging out with my own age group and always spent time with older people. I liked their opinions. It was always so much more interesting than going to Kolkata's Tollygunge Club to talk about who was making out with which girl, which was invariably where conversation with my own age group slid. I still invite a lot of older people to my parties. When I recently asked a friend for dinner, she cattily asked me, 'I hope it's not the eighty-plus crowd?' I am afraid it was a little elderly.

Older people are not competitive. More importantly, you can probe them for opinions and stories. I've always loved history and strongly believe that our future cannot be determined without us resolving the past. Look at the Commonwealth Games 2010 and the way in which we pulled it off at the very last minute. Isn't that the way Indians always study? Cram everything a week before their exams? Our past is always reflected in our present and who better to teach us than the older generation?

And now, as I am getting older, I increasingly invite younger people as well. Often you'll see my friends at an evening with their children. Sometimes you might see the kids, and not the parents. When I hosted a dinner for Arun Sarin of Vodafone recently, I invited my friend's bright young son who I thought would benefit from the party and meeting the crowd but didn't invite the parents, much to their dismay. After all, all young people need to meet interesting older people too! Most people I know stick to their age groups. One sure-fire way to gain social success and expand your circle is to stop being ageist.

Bottom line: *be interested in people, not because of how wealthy or intelligent they are or how old, but because of what they are like*. Growing up in Kolkata taught me this important lesson. Kolkata has this inherent belief in the mind over the materialistic and there, social hierarchy was not about how wealthy you were but how bright. This has stayed with me. If you can hold on to this principle, you'll see all sorts of people enter your life and you'll be amazed by how much fun you're having with them. After all, the essence of life—and a good party—is unpredictability. Now this may seem to be contradictory as I said I have the same people at my parties; it is not. Allowing people to enter your lives is different from allowing them into your home. And remember, having people home is when they are special to you: the essential difference between friends and acquaintances I would imagine.

That's what tires me about many parties I attend. I always know what to expect. At my parties, even I am not sure of what to expect. I have over the years been asked to host many parties for people because my parties have a sense of surprise about them. Nothing delighted George Osborne, the current British Chancellor of the Exchequer and a recent guest, more than to rub shoulders with the author William Dalrymple on the one hand and a diamond-laced Vijay Mallya on the other. He may have met the latter at some silly state dinner but would he have met the former?

Now, Rule 3 is actually connected to Rule 1. The simplest way to connect with different people is to have different interests. The actor Roshan Seth is a dear friend and a regular guest at my parties. We met at a theatre reading and instantly hit it off (both of us also share a passion for being punctual and Roshan is inevitably my first guest at all my dinner parties). The lawyer Raian Karanjawala and I share a love for luxury items like watches, drink and good food. I am still close to one of my oldest school friends, Anil Pathak, because of a shared love of playing pranks. They're all friends for different reasons and when all of them are at a party, they make it interesting because of how different they are. You must try to cultivate a similarly varied circle of friends.

Finally, don't judge anyone harshly simply because they dislike you. Remember, Churchill said that the only person you need to be popular with is your wife. (Thankfully I am a bachelor!) I am often referred to as obnoxious, rude, and arrogant by an army of people who don't even know me. Do I care? Not at all. I know I have been fair and ethical and as for the rest, they can think whatever they wish. They are neither paying my bills nor am I marrying them. If someone dislikes you, then it's his or her problem. Let them deal with it. There is no point fretting about it or trying to 'make up' as it were. Just ignore them and move on.

MY MANTRAS

•

Judge people humanly;
not by their wealth, status,
intelligence, or politics.

•

Mix up the guest list
at your parties.

•

Don't judge those who
dislike you.

RULE 4

The trust rule

(never pass on the bitching)

WHAT THIS RULE WILL TEACH YOU

- How to praise people effectively
- How to bitch with sincerity
- How to deal with gossip

The Trust Rule is critical and you will always get judged by it if you either move around (or wish to) in haloed circles. Don't ever do, what I call, third-party bitching, that is, meet someone and tell them the gossip you've heard about them. Most of us don't do this out of malice. Often we do it unconsciously, as a way to create a bond with a person. 'You know X said such and such about you,' is said with the subtext, 'I am trustworthy and am telling you this to help you; X on the other hand isn't all that kosher so beware.' You couldn't be more wrong.

There is always a desire among people to ingratiate themselves with cliques or groups by indulging in negativity. We are easily tempted to exhibit either proximity or power by telling people what is being said about them. In this way, we inevitably become carriers of mindless conversation. None of this is necessary. It may endear you to some but remember, even those people will probably look at you with suspicion (though they may never show it) and will ultimately not trust you. Gossip and bitching are some of the key factors of creating distrust amongst people and *one of the key factors to creating friendships is establishing trust.* People must trust you and you need to do the same without colouring the relationship with hearsay, malice, or gossip. Otherwise you can never be friends.

So I always follow a simple rule, which I recommend you do too. If I have heard X bitch out Y, I never mention it to Y. But if X has complimented Y, I always make sure to pass that on. First, it keeps your relationship intact with both parties. More importantly, if you pass on the good, it establishes your credentials. It makes you seem more reliable and the consequence of this is that it makes you better liked. Goodwill spreads and in the process positive messages spread. Ultimately, *it is more important to charm people with knowledge and humour than to seem powerful with negativity*.

SUB-RULE 1

Defend your friends

Always draw a line about bitching a friend out. I would go even further and say that *you must defend friends publicly* and not put up some mild, half-hearted defence but a vigorous, uncompromising one at that. This shows you are loyal, trustworthy, and caring; all attributes that you need to be associated with and qualities that will help you attract more friends. Recently during the 2G scam, I passionately defended my clients, the Tatas, both privately as well as on television. I got pilloried for doing so, both in my social circle as well as in social media. I did not keep quiet. I retaliated with facts. Silence is often misconstrued as guilt or weakness, so don't be silent if you are convinced about your beliefs. To briefly recap, the Tatas were accused of complicity with A. Raja on the 2G licences. But the Tatas never got one single licence either through Raja's tenure or during his predecessor Dayanidhi Maran's tenure but then the Tatas were too decent to make too much of a noise or for that matter even manipulate the media. The tragedy is that to this day, Tata Docomo does not have spectrum even in principal cities such as Delhi. The Tatas' stand was vindicated first by Telecom Minister Kapil Sibal, who went on record to mention how the Tatas had been deprived and then later, the CBI (Central Bureau of Investigation) exonerated the Tatas of any wrongdoing. In my heart, I knew all along that they were clean and unblemished and I had no hesitation (and never will) in standing up for them. We need iconic groups in a country which is littered with scamsters.

There have been many instances when people have spoken to me about some of my dearest friends and expected me to react. They expect agreement, whereas I always do a 180 degree turn and defend my friends to the hilt. This is not just a trick or a tactic to get ahead in life.

When the Niira Radia tapes surfaced, there was much debate on Barkha Dutt in the social circuit. Now Barkha is someone I have known for years and her integrity is above reproach. I had to hear many people bitch her out but I would stand up for her and I continue to do so at every opportunity. *When you make friends, make them unconditionally*. If you don't, then you will fall into a trap of taking convenient stands and this is the mistake many of us make. We defend or attack people based on what we can get out of them at that moment, rather than doing it out of an emotional attachment. Care for your friends, and show that you're a loyal friend. I don't mean paying lip-service but going that extra mile and letting people know that they can count on you if they ever need help, privately or publicly.

SUB-RULE 2

Bitch with conviction

Having said that, you do need to take a stand against people who you believe are unethical or have done something wrong. But when you do take this kind of stand, make sure you aren't just bitching (although to many it may come across thus) but that it is a view you believe in with conviction (go back to Rule 2).

There are many powerful and important-for-business people that I have spoken against. And many a time I have been told by friends that it is just not worth it. So does one have to speak out? Should one stick one's neck out? I don't really know about what others feel but given the fact that I am in some sort of public space, I feel it is imperative I take a principled stand: which does not succumb either to popular recourse or for that matter to business reasons. Consistency of a stand is reflective of the values you believe in and will stand for. It is not about taking on the world as a messiah. It is just about being honest to yourself and ensuring you are not being a hypocrite. Eventually, we are all about our beliefs and values. So take a stand if you have the courage to see it through and you will realize how much of a difference it really makes. People will respect you for that. Not deride you.

I recently spoke (and wrote) against both Rajat Gupta and Anil Kumar who brought great disrepute to not just themselves, but to the venerable consulting house, McKinsey, when they were indicted for insider trading in New York. It was a tough stand to take because we share many common friends, including some who are my clients. But taking a stand is different from mindless bitching and this is the distinction you must learn to draw. This seems tough but is easily done when you know right from wrong and make up your mind to act according to the values you hold dear. As I've said before, wearing your opinions proudly will only foster appreciation for you among others.

.... SUB-RULE 3 ....

A bitch is a boomerang

Not everyone will have such a principled view of what can be said about people and you will, in all likelihood, find yourself the butt of someone's bitching sooner or later. This is especially likely to be the case if you're successful. People *will* bitch you out. That is the nature of the beast. You will be discussed (either well or poorly) only if you've done something that is considered worth talking about. No one discusses their domestic staff, unless of course they've run away with your spouse or your money, in which case they too have done something. People only discuss those who are in the public eye, are successful or influential, preferably all three. So never get ruffled by what people say about you, either to your face or behind your back. You have to have a thick hide. The more you let it get to you, the more it will happen.

I learnt this lesson from the not-so-wise politician, Amar Singh, when he once told me how unfazed he was with media criticism of him. He said, in Hindi, that it is always important to be in 'parcha, charcha, and kharcha', which, simply put, means you must always be written about, be spoken about in social circles and be able to afford to pay for your own cup of tea or drink. It is a banal thought if you hear it for the first time but if you analyse it, Amar Singh's philosophy is actually very deep. The reality is that there is no way to stop people from bitching you out. That's the way of the world. Krishna bitched out Arjuna's cousins to him in the *Mahabharata*. Kaikeyi poisoned many a mind in the *Ramayana*. Bitching goes as far back as our mythical legacy so we shouldn't be denying its existence. We just need to keep ourselves away from it and live happily. And I guess it will be a while before someone can separate 'bitching' from 'taking a stand' and this is the debate.

....

Now, here are my ultimate secrets for dealing with bitching. If you want to find out whether someone is a bitch, tell him or her something you haven't told anyone. Sooner rather than later, the story will boomerang back to you, most likely misquoted, if the person has talked.

Once you discover that you are the object of gossip, take instant action. If my friends come up and tell me they've heard that I have been saying nasty things about them, my response is simple and immediate. I grasp the bull by its horns and insist that we discuss this one on one or in a conference call with the gossip who has said this of me. With friends, one should put a stop to these Chinese whispers as soon and as decisively as possible. As I have said before, relationships are about trust, and gossip and bitching are great destroyers of that fundamental of friendship.

If you have bitched someone out, and if someone confronts you, be honest. Many years ago, in *The Indian Express* I wrote an article listing the top ten among the most boring people in Delhi and one of the names I included was politician Subirammi Reddy. The very next day, I happened to bump into him at a dinner and he confronted me. All I did was smile and deflect his anger by saying a lot of people had called me on that article and said I had been too harsh. So at one fell swoop, I negated his anger with harmless flattery and we've remained friends (though I still do find him boring).

Bitching isn't the only thing that erodes trust. So does praise. Too often compliments can become flattery and flattery puts you in an asymmetrical relationship with a person. Compliments, as we all know, can be very disarming. If delivered in the right way, there is nothing more powerful. The trick is to praise people for something they've done well without coming across as a sycophant (as you read on, you'll see the importance I place on equality in friendships). The way to do this is to have a proper and distinctive reason for praising a person. This is what I call 'effective flattery'. To return to the trust factor, giving people a reason for you praising them makes them feel as if they haven't been complimented as much as told the truth about themselves.

Another great tactic is to compliment people for unusual reasons. There is no point telling Vijay Mallya that he is an astute businessman. He knows that. What will make him happier is if you tell him he has great taste in art and women (though perhaps not necessarily in that order) because this is something few tell him. Similarly, there's no point in telling a lawyer he has a fine legal mind. But yes, if you can compliment him on his taste in furniture, for instance, he will appreciate that a lot more because it shows you're paying attention to more than the façade.

My other rule about praise is to always praise people behind their backs and criticize them to their face.

We always do the reverse, which is why there are problems in people's relationships. Praising people behind their back is the opposite of bitching them out. They will believe it more and remember the good things you say when someone else tells them how much you appreciate their qualities.

MY MANTRAS

•

Always defend your friends, publicly and privately.

•

Accept that you will be maligned, especially once you begin to do well.

•

Praise people behind their backs and bitch about people to their faces.

RULE 5

The conversation rule

(don't try to impress people)

WHAT THIS RULE WILL TEACH YOU

- How to talk in a way that makes maximum impact

- What to never bring up in public situations

- The importance of being a good listener

There's a work dinner to which you've been invited and you've been seated next to the sales director of the company. This is your big chance to impress him. How do you do it? I get asked variations of this question all the time. You know what my answer is? I don't believe in love at first sight. People never need to be impressed. If you are smart and worthy, it will happen eventually. Let me assure you that the harder you try and impress people, the more they will be unimpressed.

However there is a corollary: you may never impress a person in the short term but you can wow them in the long term by being consistently intelligent, thoughtful, and by holding on to your opinions. My dear friend Mala Singh, the publisher of *Seminar*, once said to me that I was the only person in the country who had any balls. She was reacting to something that I had said that evening on television and the reason I raise this is that I know Mala loves me because I am forthright. More recently, on this whole Baba Ramdev fast issue, I stood behind the government and was pilloried on television and twitter but I loved what Mani Shankar Aiyar said to me post one of those debates: he said, 'I now know you speak your mind and you are brutally honest.'

Mani and I have crossed swords all our lives: for him to say this while rushing into the studio gladdened my heart. My dear friend Pavan Varma, author and diplomat, once said in an interview to Nikhil Khanna, who was doing an article on me for *Man's World*, that one of my qualities was my ability to write. Now, that was a comment I loved, particularly because it came from a man of Pavan's intellect and craftsmanship. You have to earn people's trust and admiration. That's why we're friends. So keep in mind that there's a difference between impressing in the short term and creating a lasting impression. Try and work on the latter. That is what will help you go far. The former is very short-lived and people move on.

Also, no matter what anyone says, there's never a sure-fire way to impress someone. It's ultimately what the other person feels about you and you can't control that. Russi Mody was the first influential and older friend I made. I've talked about him earlier. I met him at my friend Gita Kumar's eighteenth birthday. We were both interested in opera and food. He was a literature and humanities student like me. As he famously said to many, he was an 'MBW', a master at the business of walking around.

Those were not the days of Google where you could immediately research one another by logging on to the Internet. I didn't really know who he was and we became friends unselfconsciously, drawn to each other by our common interests. When people come to see me, they often remark that they've 'Googled' me, thinking I will be impressed or perhaps flattered. I am neither. Google hampers social interaction because we know so much more about other people without interacting with them and consequently, we then don't approach them as equals. What's worse, we meet them with preconceived notions, which is again silly.

My friendships with Khushwant Singh and R.K. Laxman were equally natural. I met Khushwant in 1981, when I was working on a book on Kolkata. I sought an appointment from him and then went across to his home at Sujan Singh Park to meet him. We got talking and one thing led to another. Not only did he agree to work with me on the book, he also recommended me to R.K. Laxman, the cartoonist, whom I then went and met in Mumbai.

Laxman and I became friends and have remained thus ever since. We've taken holidays together;

we've drunk Old Monk rum together and chatted about the world with one another. People often ask me why a man of either Khushwant's scholarship or Laxman's acumen would want to spend time with someone like me. I don't know. All I can say is, when I first met them, I did so as an equal. I did not approach them as if I was in awe of them and over the years, I have treated them with affection and respect. People want to be treated with dignity and affection, especially those who are powerful and accomplished. A lot of the time, people treat celebrities with respect but the affection is missing and that shows. When R.K. Laxman was given the CNN-IBN Lifetime Achievement Award, I went up to his suite and brought him down to the venue. I could have easily not taken the trouble of wheeling him around. After the event, I went up to his suite and we had dinner together. This is affection because this is what they least expect and most deserve.

Have I just made things harder for you? Well then, let me help you out a bit. If you are sitting next to the boss and want to impress him, learn to cultivate two things: having an opinion (we've covered this already) and being witty. Of all the talents in the world, a sense of humour is the most important. I was once chairing a session about art in the *India Today* Summit with Sonny Mehta, the legendary publisher of Knopf, and Aishwarya Rai. The hall was obviously packed and Sonny was a bit uncomfortable because he knew the power of Bollywood. So I began by saying, 'Ladies and gentlemen, I am delighted with Delhi's intellectual capacity—that each one of you has come to hear Aishwarya and see Sonny.' The house collapsed in laughter and we had a session laced with wit and merriment. It also made both Sonny and Aishwarya feel instantly at ease. People want to be amused and they don't enjoy malice or silence. Both are persona destroyers. But wit is a talent and like all gifts, not available to all of us, in which case you are best going back to the Impact Rule.

If you can summon up neither humour nor debate, fall back on the safest and most civilized option: *ask people about themselves. It always works.* How is their family? Did the older boy's exams go well? What was the pilgrimage they took last month like? Should you be taking it too? Ask about holidays and if the person is young and wild, like my dear friend, columnist Bhaichand Patel, then ask about the latest women. You have to remember we live in a world where it is all about 'me, myself and I'. It is not about you. So if you are able to probe people on their beliefs, their views and their life, you'll be the winner and you wouldn't have even revealed your cards (or life) to them. *The ultimate weapon in a party is not your Cartier watch or your Gucci shoes; it's your pair of ears.* Great listeners are the ones whom people love because they always have so much to say to them. So become a listener and see your social life change. People will be impressed by you without your trying too hard.

.... SUB-RULE 1 ....

No-no topics

I have always steered clear of a few topics at a party. I never talk about sex or gossip, about who's sleeping with whom (see the Trust Rule). Word always gets back because this is the most salacious topic of discussion and inevitably you will be blamed for talking about such things or worse still, get cornered by various folks the morning after. It is just not worth it.

Never talk about religion. It is a private matter and must remain so. I will never discuss any religion disparagingly because it is impolite and does not make for a comfortable ambience. Religion, especially in India, can be a pretty inflammatory subject and is best avoided at social get-togethers.

I never talk about money or for that matter, ask someone how much they've made or how much they spent on their brat's wedding. Such personal questions don't concern us and we don't need to come across as inquisitive. If someone wants to brag, they will. They don't need you to incite or provoke them.

Illness and disease are other topics I always avoid. If my friend has an illness in the family, I will speak to him or her privately but will not holler about it in front of a hundred people. I have seen many louts who will ask people publicly about how their mother is coping with cancer or some such sensitive question. You think you are being caring but in reality you are just being indiscreet.

SUB-RULE 2

Stay on the fringes

If there's ever an argument at a party in which you're involved, never take the side of the important guy. Be neutral. The other day Arun Jaitley and Rajdeep Sardesai had a heated argument at one of my dinners. I stayed out of it. I am not a great reconciler so why should I step in? The other thing is, never get involved in a family quarrel. *Never take sides in a battle between family members, particularly between brothers and/or a husband and wife.* It is bad karma and what's more, they could easily turn around and go after you, making you seem like the troublemaker. What's the point?

But, remember, ultimately the only way to make an impression is to be consistent, decent, and intelligent over a period of time. You must never walk into a party thinking it's a transaction. You walk into a party to have fun, make merry and at the most, to build an alliance. Many of my friends come to my parties to have a good time, not to socially work the system. So the last thing they want is some young Turk trying too hard to impress them. There have been many instances when I have had to drop the compulsive networker or business seeker from my guest list for the simple reason that I do not want my guests to feel uncomfortable and hounded when they are at my home. *The powerful are very fragile. They see more into actions than we would.* So even if you don't mean to be 'pushy', they may very well believe you are. So the best thing to do is to drop the whole act of pushing your CV and enjoy the party. If you do, you (and they) will feel good and if you get to meet another time, you won't be recognized as the annoying guy from the last party.

MY MANTRAS

•

Don't Google someone you're about to meet. It makes your interaction feel unnatural.

•

The rich and powerful can be sensitive. Be careful you don't make them feel as if they're being bulldozed.

•

Wit can be a man's greatest asset, but so can having an opinion and the ability to listen.

•

Ask people about themselves.

RULE 6

The networking rule
(don't try to make important friends)

WHAT THIS RULE WILL TEACH YOU

- The difference between status and talent
- The need to be a '2 am friend'
- The rules of friendship with a VIP

Now, we come to the most important question, the answer to which I know you've all been waiting. How the hell does Suhel know so many people? What's his secret to cultivating important friends? Well here it is: the worst thing you can do is go looking for VIPs. If you follow the last few rules, you will meet a larger group of people who, hopefully, will be as bright as you are and thus be successful too.

Importance is transitory (we'll come to this later on), so *look for accomplished people, not important people*. If you look for accomplished people, you are a talent seeker; if you look for important people you are a designation seeker. Remember, the talented become important and remain relevant. Rajdeep Sardesai and Arnab Goswami, both of whom head two very prominent TV news channels, are very dear friends of mine. They were news anchors when I first met them and I became friends with them because they would invite me to speak on some of their shows. Rajdeep and Arnab are also self-made, like most of my friends. I don't worship my friends' riches but I do worship their accomplishments and talents. If I were you, I wouldn't be eyeing the boss; I'd make a beeline for that bright young executive who always makes a smart point at every meeting, or the unknown journalist who writes the funniest stories, or the rookie ad filmmaker who dreams of becoming the next Raju Hirani or Dibakar Bannerjee. These are the people with the ticket to the future. I was always sure my friend Ashoke Viswanathan, who directed me as Bhutto in the play by the same name, would one day become one of India's finest directors. Not once did I refuse to act with him or be part of any of his plays. It is this belief in a person's abilities that you must harbour, irrespective of where the person stands at the moment.

If you were to strip my philosophy down to its barest essential, this would be it: aim always to *make friendships, not contacts*. People can't be names on a business card for you to collect. To be truly well connected, you need to make relationships, find people you care for and who care for you. *The key is not to see networking as something that is simply transactional. If you take that approach, you will never succeed in making genuine friends.* My famous friends are first my friends, and I am committed to them (remember the Trust Rule).

Friendships require investment. Start by meeting people and asking yourself if you like them enough to want to be their friend. Do you enjoy talking to them? Do you have things in common with them? Are you willing to give them time and attention, to be, what I call, their '2 am friend'? Someone who is there for them no matter what or when. Do you understand and relate to what they like or don't like? Lastly and crucially, are you happy when they do well? I have always been genuinely happy for friends who have become successful. They're my friends and friendship is unconditional.

On the flip side, I have plenty of enemies because of my strong likes and dislikes. Some of these are very important people. I don't give a toss about how powerful these people are but if they have done things in my presence that I don't respect then I don't want them in my house. So bottom line, when you're looking to make friends, focus on yourself—who you are, your interests and beliefs, your likes and dislikes—as much as the other person's status.

F. Scott Fitzgerald famously said that the rich are different. I disagree. *There's no special VIP DNA.*

The rich are just like the rest of us. But there are a few things you need to keep in mind.

At the heart of any friendship lies equality and the key to a friendship with someone wealthier and more influential than you is to keep your parity. I share my feelings and opinions freely with my friends (a little too freely, some might say). But the point is that I am never anyone's courtier. Some of my friends may have more money and power but I always feel equal to them. That's why we're friends. And this is the secret to my relationships with so-called important people: They like me for my straightforward, tell-it-like-it-is approach. Or perhaps they need a court jester, which is a role I'm fine with too. But the one thing I have steered clear of is becoming a groupie or part of any clique. I have many clusters of friends since I have many interests and I'm happy to be this way.

.... SUB-RULE 1 ....

Lowest common denominator

Because I believe in equality, I've also looked for the lowest common denominator in friendships.

This means looking for the simplest qualities that you share with the person, and not focus attention upon the type of house they live in or the brand of car they drive. People don't have to be bought with champagne and caviar, or expensive meals at five-star hotels. You're likely to share more when you both talk about your love for cricket or savour a good biryani. I, for one, am easily bought by mutton curry and I never get carried away with lavish preparations at my dinners (more on this in the Appendix). My dearest friends Pavan and Renu Varma serve delightful mutton curry at their home and that dish has been as much a cement for our friendship as my respect and affection for the two of them.

....

The rich are looking for honesty, not agreement. They will invariably know if you are sucking up to them because you're certainly not the only one doing so. I've always given back as good as I've got and, as you can guess by now, held on to my opinions. Some of my friendships have in fact become closer because I have challenged my friends. When I first met William Bissell of FabIndia, for instance, we had a huge argument about the levels of corruption and what he thought of austerity (he still drives around in an Ambassador car, which is perhaps why his definition of austere is stricter than mine). But knowing him and his contribution to modern India, I realized he was right and I was wrong.

I have two rules that I follow in my friendships with important people. Both have held me in good stead and will be invaluable for you too.

.... SUB-RULE 2 ....

Don't call

When friends become important, I wait for them to call; I never call them. I cannot remember a single time when I have called Arun Jaitley or Kapil Sibal or Kamal Nath, except to perhaps invite them home for a meal. It is not about being prissy but my logic is simple. Powerful people are likely to be busy. What if I call and the person does not pick up the phone because he is genuinely busy? Would I be upset by their not taking my call? Chances are, I would be. This is human nature so it is best to avoid such scenarios and keep the rules of engagement simple and free of misunderstanding.

SUB-RULE 3

No favours

I never ask my friends for anything. In fact, I go the opposite way and always make them feel like I am doing them a favour. When I throw a party, I am always thinking of who would be the most interesting people for my friends to meet. This is what makes the time they spend in my company enjoyable, and they appreciate me for giving them that. When I threw a party for the Bachchan family a few months ago, I invited Mr M.K. Rasgotra and his wife, who are old family friends of the Bachchans but whom they hardly see any more. Both sides were extremely touched by the gesture.

Arun Jaitley once said to some people that since his ascent to power, all his friends had asked him for something or the other. All except me. I still go to the passport offices myself without pulling strings. When I breakfast with Sheila Dikshit every few months, all I insist upon is that she serve me her famous full English breakfast, with chicken sausages and the works. Few know that I had created the 'Bhagidari' concept for her and this has stood her in good stead. I have never used our time to complain about illegal bore wells or the stretch that has been dug up in Maharani Bagh (a major source of annoyance for me). We talk instead about gardens, grass varieties and flowers. Mrs Dikshit loves her gardens as do I (go back to the Self Development Rule).

....

In short, if you want to grab the attention of important people, see yourself as their equal, hold on to your opinions, and never ask them for favours.

Here are some other tricks of the trade. Always make friends with their spouse. For example, I am closer to Kapil Sibal's wife Promilla than to Kapil. While everyone who goes to Mumbai always calls Supriya Sule, Sharad Pawar's daughter, I make it a point only to call Sadanand, her husband, because he is my mate. Shashi Tharoor is my friend because his wife, Sunanda, and I have been friends for many years. *Respect the couple. Don't link yourself to the more powerful half.* This is the golden rule. Remember, it is Nyna Mittal who has the power to veto her husband Sunil's guest list. In fact, it's always the wives who handle the dinner parties. It's served me well to have been friendly with the wives and the kids. But again, this brings me back to my earlier point that if you're genuinely friends with someone, you take an interest in their families.

Having good manners always helps and is a simple way to make people feel well disposed towards you. After every dinner party, the next day I send a handwritten thank you note and in it, I mention the couple by name. In fact, I travel with my personal stationery wherever I go. In my thank you notes, I always make it a point to talk about the food and specifically mention the dishes. I'll say the biryani was particularly delicious or that the apple pie was superlative, and so on. If someone makes an effort to invite you and serve good food, you should make the effort to appreciate it as well. You may choose to send an SMS or email instead of a note (although, in my opinion, nothing beats a handwritten note on your own letter paper) but make sure you follow this etiquette. I often send a book with my note and invite the person to my home but I rarely send anything else. If you do bring a gift for your hosts or send them a thank you present later, remember one thing: gifts should be personal. They should reflect you. That's why I never send anyone big Diwali presents. They are the worst example of mass customization and invariably get recycled.

SUB-RULE 4

Tides of change

Don't forget people when they have stopped being important. As I've said earlier, fame and power are fickle things and the key is to focus on the person, not their status. Syed Shahnawaz Hussain used to be the minister of civil aviation in the NDA government. He was famous at the time for holding the most lavish iftaar parties. In spite of being invited, I did not ever go to any of his dinners then. But when he stepped down from the ministry after the UPA came to power in 2004, I decided I would go and show my support. As you can imagine, virtually no one else did. Shahnawaz had made his usual lavish preparations but the place was nearly empty. He was delighted to see me and never forgot my gesture.

Bottom line: when it comes to making important friends, the operative word is *friend*, not important.

Friendship must be unconditional and it goes both ways. You have to be genuinely interested in the other person. They need to like you too. Above all, the relationship has to be equal. Have opinions and good manners, and be both sensitive and considerate. Be interested in interesting people. Think about what you can do for them rather than what they can do for you.

MY MANTRAS

•

Focus on making relationships, not contacts.

•

Look for accomplished friends, not important ones.

•

Friendship should always be based on equality.

•

There is no such thing as VIP DNA.

RULE 7

The work rule

(make friends out of clients, not clients out of friends)

WHAT THIS RULE WILL TEACH YOU

- How to handle a client
- How to treat a work relationship
- How to turn a professional relationship into friendship

If you've been carefully absorbing everything I've said so far, then this rule will seem self-evident. Never make clients out of friends, make friends out of clients. You might think this is a completely counter-intuitive rule. After all, surely the whole point of being networked is to be able to leverage it, right? Wrong.

When you begin to think about all your friends as potential clients, your entire mechanism for befriending someone changes. Usually clients are demanding and they have every right to be. This puts a strain on the friendship. We may feel our friends have suddenly changed as people and are no longer on our side. They, on the other hand, might feel that we aren't giving them the service they deserve as professionals and are taking advantage of the shared friendship. In the past, I've often had colleagues come to me with the complaint that they brought in a new client into the advertising business, using their friendship with the client and how their relationship has fallen apart. This is a common occurrence and I am never surprised when it happens. Work must eventually be merit driven. On the other hand, friendship is often driven by values and emotions. These two different motivations exist in their own silos.

Also, remember the last few rules. Friendships have to be based on equality. By now, you should know that this is an obsession of mine. However, in the professional world, there is a hierarchy that you cannot ignore. The telecom mogul Sunil Mittal is a friend of mine and although I could try and make him a client, I never would. The minute we're in a professional setting, he becomes the client while I lower the pedestal on which I am standing. I am an extremely proud person. I believe that the only things you should pray to God for are your continuing self-esteem and your parents' long life. Everything else is incidental. Hence, my belief that relationships have to be as equal as possible.

Turning friends into clients is a recipe for disaster as far as I am concerned. It's likely that you will lose both the friend and the client. This lesson I learnt very easily and early on. When my brother and I started our advertising agency, Equus, we went to one of our close pals, Priya Paul, hoping she would give us the contract for Park Hotels since we knew her well and because my brother had built many of the brands there. My brother created the communication for their iconic nightclub in Kolkata called 'Someplace Else' as he did with all the collaterals and the basic positioning as it were. The tonality of the communication was crafted by my brother Swapan when he was at Grey. Despite all this, she didn't give us the contract. Did we feel terrible? Of course we did, but in her own way, Priya helped us learn a lifelong lesson. *Never take friends for granted. Equally importantly, never take their business for granted.* The two are mutually exclusive, as they should be.

But here's the corollary (and this is the real meat of this rule, as far as I'm concerned): try and make friends out of clients. Both Analjit Singh of Max India and Kingfisher's Vijay Mallya became friends after becoming clients. If clients become friends, it solidifies the relationship. After all, it's because they value your advice that a friendship develops.

So, how do you turn your professional acquaintances into friends? First, remember that your initial dealings with them should be absolutely clean. For example, I have never charged tobacco and alcohol bills at a hotel to the client when I'm staying at their expense. I will never charge the client for any dinners or lunches that I have not had in my room. This also means I will not be inviting the whole world and running up an enormous bill. Why charge my client for something that has nothing to do with the work that I have come to do?

The client must know that you are not someone who will take advantage of them. When they become your friends, little things like this can irk them. Once, a client asked a colleague of mine why he was charging laundry to the client organization and I couldn't resist jumping in on my colleague's behalf and saying because we didn't want to wash our dirty linen in his boardroom. The bother stopped immediately.

Second, I make sure work is strictly work. I have never wooed a client unprofessionally. Never taken them to fine restaurants, never bestowed expensive gifts on them, and never offered any inducements to seduce them into working with me. Nor do I usually do so with existing clients. The line demarcating the professional from the personal should be clearly drawn.

Third, work hard. My clients pay me for my advice and my job is to give them the best service I can. If I am not on holiday, I am always available to my clients for anything they may require. Yes, anything. Sometimes I have been called for help with hospital admissions and so on, which I have always done. There have been innumerable times when I have told the client what they didn't want to hear but I've done so because I felt it would serve them well to know my opinion. Most of the time, they have respected the fact that I have stuck to what I believe is best for them. I may be wrong but my client will not (and should not) doubt my integrity and my commitment to their best interests.

Finally, let your clients come to you. Work hard for them, be forthright in your opinions and you will gain their trust. This is how clients become friends. The resulting personal relationship becomes an expression of their faith in you professionally. The secret to converting a client into a friend is that you have to be someone they trust and respect at work. Remember, it is your work that counts first with them.

R.K. Krishna Kumar, a venerable guru at the House of Tata, has been a great supporter and a mentor of sorts to me. I first met him when I was working in Ogilvy in 1990 and he was the boss of Tata Tea in Kolkata. Ogilvy had been briefed to work on branded spices that would be presented to the market by Tata Tea. I did extensive market visits and found that, at the time, no pan-Indian brand was likely to be immediately successful and that it would take two to three years to break even. If I had been the wicked kind, I could have lied or fudged my market visit reports in order to protect my agency's business but I did not. I earned Mr Krishna Kumar's trust back then, as a rookie in advertising. Many, many years later, I met Mr Krishna Kumar again and he asked me to start working with the Taj. Today, not only has Mr Krishna Kumar given me a lot of business within the Taj but also in the Tata Group. He knows he can trust me to put forth scenarios as they are and give him advice that is proper and honourable.

However, there are some sub-rules to this.

.... SUB-RULE 1 ....

Friends on top

If your client–friends walk out of the professional relationship, you must remain friends. It is very tempting to lose one's cool and say 'to hell with that bloke' but in the long run, it is not worth it. Why lose both a client and a friend when you can lose just one? Friendship is ultimately more important than business. As I keep saying, relationships need investment but where relationships are different from stocks and shares is that if you are in a relationship, you cannot measure it by the 'return on investment'. If you do, you are dead. If you have made such an investment in your clients and they in you, why lose it over business? You should have gone past it. Vijay Mallya stopped working with Equus, my old ad agency, but our friendship has remained as strong as ever. The truth of the matter is neither he nor I have ever discussed Equus. That is history, as far as I'm concerned, and history is a country where no one lives.

SUB-RULE 2

No work during after hours

You can only make friends out of clients if you don't discuss work outside the office. Remember, work ends in the office. If you are unable to manage this distinction, then you should keep clients as clients. Analjit and Vijay often come home but when they do, we talk about other things. With Vijay, the subjects tend to be politics, global trends, women, cars, and, the latest films. Analjit is perhaps one of the most attention-to-detail oriented people I have ever met. He makes hotelier and owner of the Oberoi group of hotels–Biki Oberoi look like a school kid. He and I chat about various things, from trends in alternate healing to new business ideas to life habits and so on. Hero Honda MD, Pawan Munjal became a client and then a friend. Today, he is someone whose opinion I value on things other than work. He is an authority (not on two-wheelers, as you'd expect) but on cars and, believe it or not, on luxury holidays and cruises.

SUB-RULE 3

Only connect

I always try and put various clients together if I think they will suit one another. When I was consulting NDTV on their lifestyle channel, I suggested they pair up with Kingfisher. Thus was born the channel NDTV Good Times. NDTV found their sponsor and it was an incredible branding opportunity for Kingfisher. Both were grateful to me for finding them a win-win situation. More recently, I got the Taj to host a cocktail reception for Nobel laureates staying at the Rambagh Palace for the Jaipur Literature Festival. I gave Taj the idea of naming cocktails after these famous authors and the hotel got autographed copies of all their books to be placed on a special shelf. *Getting two groups together, where both benefit, is good business and good karma (see the Consolidation Rule for more)*. Do it if you can, and you will reap a multitude of rewards as time goes by.

A relationship cannot be a façade for something else, so don't muddle it with work or muddle work with play. Remember, clients will always have a shorter life span than friends. Go for the latter as often as you can. If the former happens, it is a bonus but not something that should drive you.

MY MANTRAS

•

Play it clean at work, so don't charge your company or your client for extras.

•

Never woo your clients.

•

Try and connect your clients as much as possible.

•

Remember that clients have a shorter life span than friends.

PART THREE

HOW TO KEEP YOUR FRIENDS

This book is essentially about the art of making friends but as we near the end, I'd like to give you two quick rules about how to consolidate friendships once you've formed the relationship. Remember, maintaining a friendship requires as much investment as creating it. It is not about trivialities like remembering a birthday or a wedding anniversary. It is much more. It is about giving them the feeling you are always there for them, in need and at play. That is the real test of valuable friendships.

RULE 8

The consolidation rule
(always help if you can)

WHAT THIS RULE WILL TEACH YOU

- To maintain your friendships
- The importance of being helpful
- Why it pays to be generous

Folks, we're near the end and by now you should have a number of weapons in your armoury and plenty of interesting new friends, as a result. But beware, it takes just a single conversation, just a brief moment, to break a friendship. We expect a lot out of our friends and they expect a lot out of us. So in the following rule, I want to focus on some of my strategies on how to strengthen your relationships.

SUB-RULE 1

Don't get territorial

My friend, lawyer Raian Karanjawala, often says that I have introduced him to three times as many people as he has introduced me to, in spite of the fact that he's supposed to be the connected guy! The thing is, I have a simple belief: *help people become friends rather than enemies*. It is easy to create enemies and even easier to get people to fight with one another. I know of a former editor who specialized in this and one fine day he was ostracized by all of Delhi. He is not an evil soul but his life's mission was to create enemies and one day he became his own biggest enemy. Was that worth it? Obviously not.

Connecting people is a very useful thing. In fact, I would say it is an art that you must cultivate and if you are able to master it, be proud of this. Ask yourself how many people have befriended each other thanks to you. Helping people make friends won't just give you karma points, it will also give you the tag of being useful and valuable. That's the best kind of soft power there is. *The more indispensable you are to someone, the stronger it makes your relationship.* Most people are insecure about themselves and their own abilities. They mistakenly believe that if they introduce someone important to another person, then they will be cast by the wayside. Wrong. That rarely happens and if it does, there is no point in being bogged down by it. You have to be large-hearted about this. One of the things people will always respect you for is your ability to get them to meet interesting and like-minded people. I know that this has always been one of the secrets of my success in social circles.

SUB-RULE 2

Help people, always

I have never shied away from helping people and I have done all kinds of things as a result. I did a quick calculation as I sat writing these pages and came to the conclusion that, on an average, 60 percent of my time has been consumed by what the world would call 'non-essential activity'. I have sat with neighbours discussing the ill-effects of the Okhla incinerator and the damage it will cause to the environment; I have sat with Yameer Adhar and Karan Bedi, children of friends of mine, discussing their business plans and so on. I don't have to do this but I like doing it. It is my way of giving back in whichever measure I can.

If people believe you can help, that alone should make you feel good. No one seeks a favour without feeling a lump in their throat, so if they are asking you for something (and it should be ethical and above board), then they are doing so because they need the assistance and have belief in your abilities. So why be either prissy or unhelpful? Look at it as a gift from God. Imagine yourself as his agent to help people.

Help can take many forms. I have a dear friend based in London, Amin Jaffer, who is an authority on Asian art and antiquities. One evening, he was home for dinner and suddenly took me aside and told me his travel agent had messed his bookings up and if I could get a room for him at The Trident for that night. The city was sold out. I made three calls, much to the chagrin of some of my guests, and made sure he got a room. What did it take me? Three telephone calls during dinner, which may have been a bit rude, but this is something that Amin always remembers and he never fails to tell people about this incident.

Being a bachelor, one would imagine I wouldn't be flooded with school and job admission requests but I am, and like how! I make sure the child or person I am recommending is someone I know well and have known for a long time. Once that has been established, I go out of my way to help only because the system is so rotten in our country. If you can put in a word for someone's kids at a good school and perhaps for a deserving job, then I feel you must do so. The good karma that will come your way is unimaginable.

The buck does not stop with me. Everyone in my office, especially my secretary Siva, has been trained to offer a helping hand to all my friends. I remember, many years ago, Rajdeep Sardesai was moving home and Siva did everything to make that move comfortable. Nowadays, there are many occasions when Rajdeep calls my direct line in office to speak to Siva rather than me. So in the process of helping, Siva too has earned admirers and friends. Another person I know who offers help easily is Karan Thapar. He is hardly the devil he is often made out to be. For example, Karan helped me get a Pakistani visa in about an hour when I was keen to watch a cricket match in Lahore. At other times, he has sent me amazing carpet-sellers and other such surprises.

But when you help, help with your eyes open and do so within the domain of honesty and decency. I receive a zillion requests from people asking me if I can get them to meet Arun Jaitley or put in a word with Prannoy Roy. I always refuse to make introductions but I do give them the office numbers. If either Arun or Prannoy or anyone else wishes to meet someone, then it is their call and while I don't want to be unhelpful, neither do I want to be blamed later, should this person be someone dubious trying to get through the door. The trick is to give the secretary's number and ask that they don't use your name. You don't want to build your popularity on the strength of someone else's name, do you?

Always remember that *the key to doing people a favour is to not expect anything in return*. Subconsciously, we are usually always hoping for something in return but the moment you do it consciously, it is all over. Remember, life is not a bargain; it's an alliance.

.... SUB-RULE 3 ....

Stay loyal

Don't go for convenient loyalty. I remember I was the only one to sign an affidavit in favour of *Tehelka* when the BJP was in power and for it, I stated on oath that *Tehelka* had no devious intent of either rigging the stock markets or bringing down a government. The government of the day, the BJP-led NDA, had charged *Tehelka* with conducting a sting operation with a view to rigging the markets. Since *Tehelka* had Shankar Sharma of First Global as their investor—he is a known bear—a lot of people bought into this theory. But this was not true. At the time, no one was willing to stick their neck out for the newsmagazine. I did it because it was the right thing to do *and* because the editor Tarun Tejpal, who is my friend, had asked me to. Stick with your friends even when the going is rough. If you are torn between being loyal to two friends, listen to your conscience. I knew signing the affidavit would upset many in the BJP—my friend Arun Jaitley was part of the government that Tarun had attacked. But I also knew my friends would respect me for being honest. To this day, Tarun remembers what I did, as do the others who did not have the courage to speak out in favour of the truth. You must always be seen to be loyal to your friends in public. Go all out with your defence of them (see the Trust Rule).

SUB-RULE 4

Create rituals

Friendship is all about consistency. My advice would be to ritualize certain things with your friends. For example, I am always at Shekhar Gupta's home for Diwali. Ten years ago, there used to be about ten of us, including the family, for the festive evening. Now there are five hundred but for me, nothing's changed. The way they treat me, their affection and grace, has remained unaltered so why would I choose another option? Every Holi of mine is spent with Vineet Jain. I will not have it any other way. If he cares to invite me year after year with love and care, why should I be ungrateful? Whenever I go to Kolkata, which is quite often, I will always have a meal with my old colleague and dear friend Anurag Hira. I could be invited out to more important people's homes but for me, it will always be Hira who will be the most important one. After all, he is my friend and I care for that friendship. Almost every time I have visited Kolkata, I have attempted to meet Russi Mody. He is very unwell and cannot remember names or faces any longer but that doesn't matter. He meant a great deal to me at a certain time in my life and that's all that counts. The same applies to the De household in Mumbai. I always make it a point to see them whenever possible. Dilip and Shobhaa are lovely people and you are guaranteed a great evening of adda and amazing Bengali food. What else can one want?

Finally, as Winston Churchill said, yours would be a life well lived if you can count ten friends on your fingertips. Don't try and befriend the whole world because in that rush, you may lose these ten. Enjoy what you have. Respect your friends and treasure them.

MY MANTRAS

•

Do your friends favours but never expect any in return.

•

Create traditions.

•

Be fiercely loyal.

•

Always introduce friends to each other.

RULE 9

The RSVP rule

(never take the better option)

WHAT THIS RULE WILL TEACH YOU

- How to handle a situation where you have double booked yourself
- How to decide which invitation to accept
- Who to invite to a party

Now, the RSVP Rule might seem like fluff but it is not. People often ignore it at their own peril and I have seen many struck off guest lists because they think they can get away by violating this. We all live in a world where we are constantly maximizing our opportunities and our time. All that baloney about being 'networked' and 'networking with the right people' prompts us to ignore this rule or shamelessly violate it. This may well be the case with you, dear reader, who should by now be the most popular person you know. Don't let it get to your head.

The rule is simple. Take a scenario that must be familiar to all of you. You've been invited to a colleague's for dinner one Saturday night. The plan was made a few weeks before. Then, at the last minute, you get a swanky invite to a client's five star cocktail party that same evening. It sounds like a glamorous event where the chances of meeting useful people are high and so, as a good networker, you should cancel on your colleague. Right? Wrong.

Honour your commitments as much as possible, especially as you get ahead in life (which is why this rule comes so near the end). Success and popularity shouldn't blunt your good manners or your sense of what is truly important. There is always a multitude of options available to us in life. The option of being blunt versus manipulative; of being honest versus dishonest; of going with the flow or against the tide, depending upon your convictions. You want to be socially adroit but it can be a recipe for disaster if you focus only on what you think will get you ahead in life.

I have a lot of friends who 'share' evenings with their wives but their wives are not with them. What this means is that the wife goes to a certain set of parties and the husband to another just so that they can appease everyone and accept every invitation that comes their way. This is a fatal error, and in the long term, it will haunt you. Pick one invitation and go together. And I would always pick the invitation that came first. I have never cancelled on an earlier engagement but I know what it does to people's reputations. You stop being invited and then people stop coming to your home. If they still do accept your invitations, then they treat you the way you've treated them. So this whole thing about the so called better option is impolite and can prove to be disastrous.

Yet sadly, it is becoming the norm, especially in the Delhis and Mumbais of the world. I can't stand people who RSVP with a 'yes' to my dinners, but cancel at the last minute because a better option has come up. There may be a good reason the first time but if I find that someone has not turned up for a couple of my parties despite RSVP-ing yes, I strike them off my guest list. So will most people. No one wants to feel used. Nor will this kind of crass behaviour endear you to those whose homes you eventually land up in, trying to be either popular or a conformist.

I get five invitations a night and sometimes they are spread across cities. I have only two criteria for measuring the value of an invite. How close am I to the person inviting me and how special is the occasion. Many a time, the evening is a veritable mela, which you can easily avoid. To this day, thankfully, I have not judged an invitation by how rich the person inviting me is. Let me illustrate what I mean. Delhi and Mumbai have a pecking order. If Mukesh Ambani invites you and so does a school friend, whose house will you go to? Now, native intelligence may suggest the former but I would urge you to judge an invitation by the following criteria:

- Who invited you first and did you accept or regret?
- Who is more valuable to you, long term?
- Who would you regret losing as a friend and well wisher?
- Would you be able to live with yourself if you made choices based on what you will get out of whom?
- Who will treat you as a friend and who will treat you as a number?
- Who will miss you if you don't show up?

The chances are that the important guys will call mainly important people, so you'll be like wallpaper at that event. The more crucial question is, how would you define 'important'?

When it comes to parties, I follow a set of principles from which I have never wavered so far. I would recommend you do the same. I only go to one party a night and if I have to go to two, then I make sure I have dinner with the person I accepted an invitation from first. Simple.

As you should know by now, the one compromise I never make is with friends. There have been instances when the likes of a Sunil Mittal or a Mukesh Ambani have invited me and I have always told them, well in advance, that I would come just for drinks and even specified a departure time so that they know I am serious about where (and when) I am headed next. This way, there are no surprises. This civility was drilled into me in Kolkata. You are graceful and grateful about invitations received.

Of course, there are several instances when one has to party hop, like during Diwali and the wedding season for example. But it makes no sense to mark yourself present and then upset people by leaving soon after because you have to go elsewhere. It is not only insulting but also the host's wife (and as I've mentioned earlier, it is invariably the better half who truly wields social power) will inevitably notice the slight and strike you off the guest list the next time round.

If you are doing more than one party, follow these rules. Try and limit your party hopping. (I stick to two myself.) Forewarn your hosts and explain why you are leaving. This way, the hosts feel you made that effort. If you leave without telling them in advance, they feel you are choosing the better option and no one wants to be belittled or feel less important than someone else.

If you are really conflicted about your social calendar, run through the criteria I have mentioned earlier. The answer will become crystal clear and I promise you, life will be a lot easier. Also, *don't see parties as work*. If you do, you'll never make the contacts you hope to. For me, parties are fun. They're a place to let loose and have a good time. Serious work never gets done on occasions such as these so if you are hoping to achieve work related stuff at a dinner and so are choosing one invite over another, think again. It never works. No one I know uses dinner parties for deal making. And as I've said earlier, work should not figure in your life after working hours.

Now for a revelation. Most people believe that the number of invitations you receive for each evening defines your popularity. Let me give you a reality check. Many a time you are a name on that list because it has been shared amongst two friends. My friend Raian Karanjawala invites everyone for his birthday dinner, and by this I mean everyone on *my* guest list as well! This gives me great joy because thanks to Raian, I can spot the freeloaders—those who don't know Raian but are happy to come and consume his alcohol and food just because they've got an invitation.

SUB-RULE 1

No anonymous invites

There is a sub-rule to be garnered from the Raian story. I have noticed a trend in Mumbai and Delhi of people inviting me to their weddings and other functions when I have never met them. I can't imagine why. Social occasions should be about friendships. I would urge you to look for quality invitations from people you love and people you know and invite only people whom you know. There is no point in attending a wedding where you know no one. Or in throwing a party and finding yourself surrounded by strangers.

SUB-RULE 2

Just say no

Never be coy or embarrassed about not being invited. I have seen many people obfuscate when asked if they are attending a particular dinner. I, on the other hand, simply say I have not been invited. It doesn't make me any smaller. But at least I do not have to spin a needless yarn.

MY MANTRAS

•

Look for an invitation that will give you joy, not stress.

•

In case of a clash, attend the invitation that you accepted first.

•

Look for recreational, and not transactional, evenings.

•

An invitation card is not a reason to draw out your visiting card.

•

Be graceful with people who
make the effort to invite you.

•

And remember, at homes
of important people,
you are unlikely to be the
important guest.

PART FOUR

IN CONCLUSION

We've come to the end of the book and I've said all I had to say. I've given you all my hard-earned wisdom, let you into the tricks of the trade, and, hopefully, given you much to chew on. So my final rule is going to be a bit of a cheat rule, a distillation of all the others that came before. But do pay attention because this is the foundation of all the rules that have come. And, as a goodbye present, there are some tasty titbits for you in the Appendix.

RULE 10

The summing up rule

(it's all about values, not valuation)

WHAT THIS RULE WILL TEACH YOU

- The pillars of social success
- The need for EQ—or the enjoyment quotient

Ultimately, social success rests on two pillars: respect and trust. The only way you can achieve this is by focusing on values and not valuations. Don't judge someone by their bank balance, social stature, and influence. Judge them by what they believe in and how they behave. Treat them accordingly and you will reap the dividends. Remember this one simple rule: *there is no point sucking up to the rich because they are not going to leave their money behind to you or me.* It is their money.

This is my favourite rule and one that keeps me grounded in reality (or at least I hope it does). But, easy as it may be to write down, it's extremely difficult to follow, especially in times such as these when we are evaluating everything on the basis of scale and size. How big is the house? How big is the car? How big is the bank balance? But we never ask, how big a heart does a person have? Does he give back to the community? Is he big on taking care of his employees and family members?

We no longer care about someone's value system. We see people only through the prism of wealth and are slowly becoming victims of valuations, rather than believers in values. This is not just sad but also self-defeating. As a concept, valuations are an external judgement of your capacity and worth. Values are what lie within and once we recognize this, only then will we appreciate how much more there is to this world than just money. Understand this and you will develop the skill of measuring people for what they really are. As I have said before, *social success depends on your ability to make friendships and relationships that are genuine.*

.... SUB-RULE 1 ....

Same same, not different

Remember always that the rich and powerful ultimately want the same things as the rest of us. I was once told by a friend of mine that at a certain stage of success (he mentioned a figure of Rs 20 crores in the bank) one's life and Mukesh Ambani's could be just the same in terms of 'EQ', or 'enjoyment quotient', as he calls it. With that kind of money, one can wear the same kind of clothes as Ambani or have the same car, although we may never have a house like Antilla or the fleet of jets that he possesses.

The larger point my friend was making was that one could have the same level of enjoyment as

Mukesh Ambani without having the same amount of wealth as he does. Two people with disparate incomes can still possess the same EQ. Ratan Tata, in an interview to the *Economist*, once said that all he looks forward to at the end of the day, is a 'good night's sleep'. He's really saying the same thing, just in a different way. All of us ultimately want a night of calm, peaceful, guilt-free sleep. We are all equals despite our trappings. Remember this always.

....

To the outside world, I may be a successful person with influential friends but as I hope you'll have noticed by now, I choose my friends because of our shared values, not on the basis of a cynical valuation of their assets. My friends aren't just 'contacts' from my little black book. They are people I love, to whom I am committed to (as I said before, *always be a 2 am friend*) and whom I admire.

No matter how powerful or influential a crook is, you should realize that you can never have him as your true friend. So keep it at an acquaintance level. My simple belief is, *never go to someone's home if you don't respect them, no matter how socially relevant or influential they may be.* You should do the same too.

Lastly, don't take the better option. Never ever dump friends because they are not important in your scheme of things. That is not why they are or became your friends. Friendship is not a bargain. It is an alliance of values and souls. Take my dear friend, Arun Sarin, the former global CEO of Vodafone (he was a client first and became a friend later). He and his wife will travel all the way from their home in California to attend every family function in Delhi and not as mere tokenism. If they're at the function, then they will be thoroughly involved and will participate in all activities. They never take their family for granted. I have often seen many make the mistake of doing so as soon as they reach a level of success. Often, the first set of people someone takes for granted is their family.

SUB-RULE 2

Old versus new

Never give precedence to your new friends over your childhood friends. Your childhood friends are the only ones who will never judge you for what you have become or when you've failed. They are the ones who will also keep your head on your shoulders. As I have said before, I never subtract from my guest list. I keep my old friends and add to that.

....

The doors to every home will be open to you once you free yourself from a life of valuation. After all, while some of getting ahead in life is about being smart and purposeful, the most important aspect is knowing that respect and love can never be bought. They have to be earned.

MY MANTRAS

•

Judge people for who they are.

•

Look at people's wealth from the human quotient perspective.

•

Keep your old childhood friends.

•

Invite people to your home who will laugh and be happy irrespective of material considerations like which car they drive or what clothes they wear.

APPENDIX

How to be a good host

1. Remember that people are coming to your house, not to a hotel. Don't go over the top with décor. Keep the ambience like that of a home and not a banquet hall.
2. In a large party, keep enough chairs for the older lot to sit.
3. Pay great attention to each guest. In your home, everyone who walks in is a VIP and everyone is special. Look after the women especially. Remember they have veto rights qua their husbands and if you treat them as furniture, the next time you'll only have furniture and no guests.
4. Make it a point to introduce everyone at your party, even if a person is famous because, as I said, everyone is special.
5. The snacks must be served as soon as the first guest walks in. There is no point starving people into fun.
6. Always, always, serve food on time. I am famous for inviting people to my home at 8.30 pm for dinner and ensuring the food is on the table at 9.30 pm, which is why when

people come to my home, they are almost always on time because they know they won't have to wait until breakfast for dinner.

7. I always present a small menu (two non-vegetarian dishes, lentils, two to three vegetarian dishes) and usually simple but good, home-cooked food. Remember point 1, don't try and be a restaurant. I also usually serve the same snacks—masala cheese toast and shammi kebabs (as I said before, keep it real). They have become a welcome tradition for my guests.
8. Eat when the others are eating. People feel happy when the host is dining with them.
9. Take great care to see off every guest at the door. Don't wish them goodbye in the drawing room. It is bad manners and terrible form.
10. Make sure you acknowledge all gifts that you receive the very next day and no, do not use a standard template. Describe the gift they gave you and thank them for it.

How to be a good guest

1. I always RSVP. Always.
2. Make sure you have not accepted another engagement when you have one already for a certain evening.
3. I never call the hosts to ask who else is going to be there. It is rude, primitive and smacks of petty networking. My belief is that I am going because my hosts have invited me and not because who else has been invited.
4. Make sure you arrive on time. This is my golden rule. If my hosts invite me for 8.30 pm, I enter their home at 8.30 pm. It is polite and since most johnnies come late, this gives me the chance to spend quality time with the hosts.
5. I start commenting on how good the home is looking from the moment I walk in and my theatre experience helps sometimes. Even if the house doesn't look as good as one would hope, I still comment favourably.
6. I am always the first one to dig into snacks. Nothing gives the host greater joy than to see his or her guests enjoy their food.

7. I am the first one to grab a plate when dinner is served. This sets the pace and every host will love you for commencing the dinner process.
8. I never look out for anyone at the party when I am in conversation with someone.
9. After the dinner, as I get into the car, I always send the hosts (both husband and wife) a text message saying thanks, and follow this up with a handwritten note the next morning. In my thank you note, I make it a point to mention the dishes and the ambience. This makes the hosts feel good and this is exactly my intent.
10. I have never ever bitched out the food or drinks at anyone's party the next day. It is bad form and despicable behaviour.
11. If I do meet the hosts the next evening at someone else's home, I never make a public statement about their party because there may be people they hadn't invited and it would only embarrass them if I mention the party in the wrong company. But I do go up to them and thank them yet again for that delicious kebab or the special mutton curry they served.

The worst social crimes you can commit

1. To arrive late.
2. To arrive at a dinner completely drunk.
3. To smoke in someone's home without seeking their consent.
4. To get into an ugly discussion on sensitive subjects like religion or sexuality or politics.
5. To insult other guests. (I have seen this happen at many parties).
6. To ask personal questions in public.
7. To get touchy feely with strangers.
8. To tell your hosts you have already eaten before.
9. To stand in one corner feeling miserable and commenting about the other guests.
10. To deface your host's home, like spilling on the carpet, putting your dirty feet on their white sofa, ashing all over and so on.

Question time

1. *My job takes me to a lot of high profile events. However, I am a shy person and am usually found in one corner looking at everyone but never quite managing to go ahead and strike a conversation. Even when I do, I get so tongue-tied that I don't know how to keep the conversation going. What should I do?*

   For starters, untie that tongue. Shy is a state of mind and not part of your DNA. If you want to do well in life, you will have to move out of that cave. Even Osama bin Laden had to move out of his cave to Abbottabad. My advice is get rid of this so called shyness by actually making conversation. The next time you are out at a party, go ahead and say something, however stupid it may be. You'll see a whole new world of stupidity open up. On a serious note, give conversation a shot.

2. *What do you do if you're seated next to someone at a dinner party who has absolutely nothing to say? Have you ever dealt with uncomfortable silences?*

   This has happened to me several times and sometimes even I can be quite stumped, and

I am by no means shy or retiring. The best way out is to look for the lowest common denominator. Say something really stupid, like discuss the flowers on the table or the lighting or even the damn weather. Something will give. If all else fails, drop a glass of wine on him or her and see the conversation flow. More seriously, you have to keep trying. Unless of course you are seated next to Shashi Tharoor, who once spent an entire evening sitting next to me, BBM-ing Sunanda Pushkar who was his lady love (not wife) at the time and I could do nothing about it. Not even a weather chat would have helped.

3. *I am twenty-seven years old. It just so happens that professionally I mostly get to deal with clients who are usually double my age and I feel some of them don't take me very seriously. What should I do?*

This is rubbish. You get taken seriously if you have something serious or substantial to say. I believe you must use your age to your advantage and if the older guy acts really cocky, then the best way to start the conversation would be with a phrase like, 'I know this is way past your generation…' and see how much rapt attention you will suddenly receive.

4. *Is it okay for me to introduce myself to a stranger in a social situation? Or does that make me seem like a creep?*

   I have always scored qua women by introducing myself to them even when I had no clue who they were, and I think this is the best way. No one will think you are a creep unless you behave like one. The reality is that people want to meet other people. My friend Raian Karanjawala is an expert on meeting strangers and converting them into family. You'll certainly find them at his birthday dinner. So if all else fails, you can always take lessons from Raian who can be found at The Chambers of the Taj Mahal Hotel every afternoon from about 1 pm to 5 pm, just when the courts are working. Incidentally, he is a lawyer.

5. *I work in public relations. The daughter of my husband's boss is pestering me for a contact of a celebrity that I have worked with. I am in a fix as neither do I want to offend her nor do I feel I know her well enough to share the information. Please help!*

Just share the information and blame it on Airtel or some other operator and say that the person must have gotten the information from elsewhere. I have a simple rule about sharing information—don't give out any private stuff. But then again, I have no boss, leave alone a husband of one so I can get away with it. Why should you come across as rude and difficult? Just give her the number and get on with it. If you really want to knife her, then tell your celebrity friend that this person was fiddling with your phone when you had gone to powder your nose and she took the number from your phone and then let that celebrity handle this gorgon. Conversely, you can follow my earlier rule about handing the public office number.

6. *What happens if my old friends and new professional acquaintances don't get along?*

   Nothing happens. Certainly no tsunami. Why must your friends and professional acquaintances ever get along? I rarely let my friends meet my professional contacts. So why would you?

7. *I happen not to have an elephant's memory and often forget people's names. It's so embarrassing! How do you deal with this?*

This is something we all face all the time and I am pretty upfront about it. I blame it on senility or jet lag or the fact that I have just recovered from a bout of piles and then go on to ask that person's name.

8. *What are your rules about romance in the workplace?*

   I have never had or encouraged romance in the workplace. It creates too many problems and there is no dearth of women so why would I mess in my own backyard? Besides, it is unethical and creates a sense of politics that frankly no one needs. I would discourage it and my advice would be desisting as far as possible. If at all you want to have something to do with someone in your office, make it an activity of lust and not love!

9. *My boss came home for dinner one evening and was rude to one of my guests. I kept quiet but now I feel guilty. Should I have done something?*

   This is a tricky one. You did the right thing but then you should have gone to him the next day and told him your guest felt miserable and that it was quite unnecessary. Or better still, the next time round, invite him and invite someone rude and ask the latter to go for your boss and just keep quiet. Your boss will get the message swiftly.

10. *I had a sit down dinner at home and when I asked my guests to come into the dining room for the meal, two of my guests didn't join us around the table and sat gossiping in the living room instead. I felt it was very rude and wondered if I should say something to them.*

    It depends how close you are to them. In my house, one of the rooms has been christened the Jaitley Room only because Arun Jaitley takes a few of my guests to that room to gossip. The good thing is everyone knows he is gossiping so if you want to join him, you know where to go and if you don't, you stay where the party is. I would not lose sleep over guests gossiping. It's better they are doing so on your terrace rather than on your neighbour's... about you!

.... ACKNOWLEDGEMENTS ....

I have many friends to thank for making me the way I am, the good, the bad, and the ugly within me that is.

SWAPAN SETH: my brother and closest friend and my constant wake-up call.

JIGME WANGDI: my schoolmate, now in the Indian Army, for keeping me grounded.

ANIL PATHAK: my schoolmate, for making me the prankster I am today.

ARUN and DOLLY JAITLEY: for showing me the sagacity and wisdom of being ethical and honest, and the advantages of being an enduring foodie.

UMA GAJAPATI RAJU and RAMESH SHARMA: for showing me Delhi and helping me settle in.

MALLIKA and JAIDIP KHURANA: for being the ones who help me fall flat to earth just when my head swells.

VIRENDER KAPOOR: for saving me from the clutches of many a stalker.

SHAHRUKH and GAURI KHAN: for showing me a Bollywood I never imagined: real and rooted.

RATNA and R.K. KRISHNA KUMAR: for teaching me the values of, well, values and principles.

Fareena and Mehli Mistry: for being my 2 am friends... I know they will always be there for me with their affection and goodwill.

Sagarika and Rajdeep: for being just simple, large-hearted, warm friends.

Shekhar Gupta and Neelam Jolly: for showing me the grace in being consistent.

Renu and Pavan Varma: for being there when I was a rookie and remaining true friends.

Raian and Manik Karanjawala: for being just who they are—one is all over the place while the other is so down to earth.

Bhaichand Patel: for showing me the future—what an old lecherous man will look like and I am perhaps on my way there.

Aveek Sarkar: for being the connoisseur he is and for keeping me interested in watches, dials, and the like.

Raj Kejriwal: for helping me sin with him without guilt and for showing me a world that I never knew existed.

Shobhaa and Dilip De: for helping me stay with the Bengali adda regimen.

Mala and Jugnu Singh: for introducing me to the world of salons and conversation.

ROMI CHOPRA and ROSHAN SETH: for being friends without malice or borders.

VIJAY MALLYA: for being the man who keeps making me think big and living life the way I do.

THE PAUL FAMILY: aunty Shirin, Priya and Sethu: for being an extension of Kolkata in Delhi.

ANALJIT and NEELU SINGH: for being the silent support system they are, more than family.

PAWAN and SUNIL MUNJAL: for teaching me the art of the understated.

SHOBHANA and SHYAM BHARTIA: for being just wonderful human beings and terrific friends and inspiring me to be one as well.

JYOTIRADITYA and PRIA SCINDIA: for taking the mickey out of me and helping me laugh all the time.

DIYA SETHI and NIKHIL KHANNA: for being weird to the point that I imagine they are for real.

CHIKI SARKAR: for being a publisher who ruled with fear but inspired with affection.

NAMRATA and A.J. SINGH: for introducing me to so many single women, all of whom, at some stage or the other, I had wanted to marry.

PROMILLA and KAPIL SIBAL: for being the couple with whom I can discuss everything and, more importantly, without fear or favour.

MEENAKSHI and HARISH SALVE: for being my passport to even greater London joys.

ANU and ANAND MAHINDRA: for their candour and their affection: never wavering, never diluted.

NITA and MUKESH AMBANI: for their endurance of my idiosyncracies and their genuine affection.

NANDAN NILENKANI: for being a refreshing breath of fresh air in an otherwise staid world.

And above all, my parents: SHUB and JOGENDRA SETH: for being part of my life like no one else can or should. For tolerating every idiosyncrasy and more…

.... A NOTE ON THE AUTHOR ....

Suhel Seth is the Managing Partner of Counselage India. Counselage is India's only strategic brand management and marketing consultancy, advising chairpersons and CEOs on branding and marketing. His clients include R.K. Krishna Kumar, Analjit Singh, Pawan Munjal, and Prannoy Roy amongst others. Suhel writes columns in the *Financial Times*, *Hindustan Times*, and *The Telegraph*. He has also co-authored two books on Kolkata with Khushwant Singh and R.K. Laxman.

A NOTE ON THE TYPE

Goudy Old Style (also known as just Goudy) is an old-style classic serif typeface originally created by Frederic W. Goudy for American Type Founders (ATF) in 1915. Suitable for both text and display applications, it is a graceful and balanced design. Goudy Old Style is considered to be among the most legible and readable serif typefaces for print.